Waysides

For the Wanderers and Listeners

poems by

Mike Matthews

Finishing Line Press
Georgetown, Kentucky

Waysides

For the Wanderers and Listeners

Copyright © 2025 by Mike Matthews
ISBN 979-8-88838-949-2 First Edition
All rights reserved under International and Pan-American Copyright Conventions. No part of this book may be reproduced in any manner whatsoever without written permission from the publisher, except in the case of brief quotations embodied in critical articles and reviews.

ACKNOWLEDGMENTS

Thank you to all who gave me the time and space to be still and listen.

The silent moment
whispers through the cracks in air—
all rests in stillness

The art in this book is all original by Mike Matthews. If there is an interest in any of the art, contact him by email: Mikdavid@hotmail.com

When I work on a painting or a poem, I practice listening to moments outside the clutter of my busy mind. When I notice a moment that sticks out of the chaos and creates its own meaningful moment, I attempt to capture that moment. To me, poetry and art do not differ by much. Words have dimension to me like the shading of an object in art gives the image a sense of space. The objects or images I illustrate seem to choose to represent the moment on their own. The images in my art and poetry manifest from the relationship I develop the medium I work with to illustrate the image. Each image reveals itself gradually to me, and after I am done, it scratches at the door to ask to be let out to find its home.
 –Mike Matthews

Publisher: Leah Huete de Maines
Editor: Christen Kincaid
Cover Art: ***Dream Cat*** Acrylics by Mike Matthews
Background Designed by Hui Qin
Interior Art: Mike Matthews
Author Photo: Hui Qin
Cover Design: Elizabeth Maines McCleavy

Order online: www.finishinglinepress.com
 also available on amazon.com

Author inquiries and mail orders:
Finishing Line Press
PO Box 1626
Georgetown, Kentucky 40324
USA

Contents

In-Breath	1
Blue Notes	2
Time's Show	3
Masque with Red Tongue	4
The Chair on the Porch	5
Birds With Apples	6
Warning!	7
Slow Motion	8
Fractured	9
Broken Cup	10
Broken up Pieces	11
Still Life with Pickled Pig Feet	12
We Believe	13
The Weeper	14
The Fresh Pomegranate	15
Lightning Storm of Insomnia	16
Two Flowers, Red and Yellow	17
Lotus	18
The Plastic Tongue	19
Money Toad	20
When History is Now	21
Squoze	22
Eyes	23
CAT	24
Blue Cat	25
Liquids	26
Bug	27
The Most Beautiful Fly in the World	28
The Prints of Nighttime	29
Spirit Fox	30
The Lost Shoe	31
A Mile in Boots (A Long Story)	32
Tucked in the Corner of Red	33
Street in China After Rain	34
The Missing Beam	35

Can Yellow See Yellow?	36
Caterpillar	37
The Day's Overtime	38
Turtles at Rest	39
A Box of Stillness	40
Harbor Moon Café	41
From Squib to Flower	42
Too Hot	43
Yawning in Yellow	44
A Toad is Home	45
Something Texas	46
The Fish Sees Me, Too	47
A Fish	48
Petals Paint the Sky	49
Symbiosis	50
A Moth Sits on its Favorite Tomato	51
Bees	52
Stinger	53
Dew Drop	54
Dare to Flame	55
The Old Gate	56
The Edge of Decay	57
A Cat Skull Full of Dead Flowers	58
The Butterfly Feast	59
Red Rabbit with Osprey Wings	60
A Wish	61
Coalescence	62
The Bike	63
Mirror	64
Money Tree	65

Waysides holds the whispers that speak through the cracks opening between minutes in motion. When I walk to the park and listen for those still moments, there may be a cat with yellow eyes inside a dark, black shape, or a sign on a telephone pole swaying in the wind while an open pipe whistles something ominous, or a broken porch in front of an abandoned and decaying house that may have held jars of sun tea. *Waysides* brings in those pebbles, splinters, fragments, distances left on the side of a steady flow of time and lays them on the page like pieces of glass that catch the light at odd angles.

—Mike Matthews

In-Breath
Acrylics: 16x20

Blue Notes
Acrylics 24 x 36

Time's Show

Mostly, time puts on a show
distracting minds with mirrors,
polished reflections of thoughts
defined as matter and concern.

Then a moment sticks out its tongue
and dissolves the illusion of time,
leaving open the beauty of stillness
so small and shining with the unexpected.

Masque with Red Tongue
Acrylics: 16x20 Canvas

The Chair on the Porch

I used to have a morning chair
where I would ask to see
what the morning would present
while I would sit and loosen
the grip of the past.

Sometimes a mockingbird
would fly from the roof
of the duplex across the street
to catch a moth only it could see
blended with the brick wall next to me.

Recently, I found a chair on the curb,
carried it up the hill, two actually,
and my arms reminded me of muscles.
This morning, the chair worked.

A young woodpecker,
with such quick agility
as if branches have no gravity,
chirped and flitted
pecking for breakfast
on the tree recovering
from snowstorms.

Birds with Apples
Pencil Drawing

Warning!

These winds whistle songs
of intertwined, organic
metal vines mixed with
slow motion transformation.
What seems fixed and solid
that holds the lines transferred
from one generator to a field
full of ground wire and houses
slowly consumes itself
back to its organic
speed of melting ice
in the dwindling heat of a sunset.

Slow Motion

Thirty seconds mark progression,
things being successfully completed,
accomplishment, transportation of materials
from where they became stored
the day before to where they
should fit the need for today—
A stillness packed full of meaning
actively restoring time and efficiency,
for the goal gives substance to emptiness
that would arise otherwise
in the void left open in the absence
of movement within the sectioned set of time.
The busy and determined seconds
speak of somewhere otherwise locked in ice:
A moment in a void of counterweight
holding together everything that should move.

Fractured
Acrylics: 16x20

Broken Cup
Alcohol Markers on paper

Boarded up Pieces

A jar full of sun tea
rested on the porch
some yesterday, didn't it?
Which hand picked it up
and poured it into memory,
left or right, and who drank it,
sweetened or unsweetened,
with or without lemon?
Someone does not desire
anyone to look behind the boards
to see the pieces of glass
on the exposed floorboards
in the space that held the dining table.
Do not pass. Do not take
what is left of the time spent
building a cohesive routine.
Behind those walls where windows
once invited the light,
there may or may not be pieces.

Still Life with Pickled Pig Feet
Acrylics: 16x20

We Believe

Ghosts exist—at least
at birthday parties
in the hearts of children
who delight in seeing
familiar heroes
who speed to their aid
with fancy and mysterious
weapons to capture
and contain the most
invisible spirits
of their darkness
and transform them
into something silly,
and they can cope with silly.

The Weeper
Acrylics: 16x20

The Fresh Pomegranate

Where would the nature
of nature go if, after a storm,
after the destructive winds,
after the recession
of the flood waters,
leaves refused to sprout,
buds decided not to bud,
and fruit remained inside the bark?
That would taste of sour fear,
like a handful of dust
under a red, red, dead rock.
Should the pomegranate emerge,
the one like itself and still a pomegranate,
it most certainly would be the pomegranate
of the new and fresh day
after the storm scrapes away
the old and dusty lenses
that covered the sunlight
of the days before.

Lightning Storm of Insomnia
Digital

Two Flowers, Red and Yellow

The red one expresses flower.
So, according to that one,
the yellow one should also be flower
in the way the red one is also flower.
After all, they are both flowers,
and being so, they should be the same
or equal to the same, according to the red one.
Yellow is fine since the red one claims
that the red one cannot see the color yellow
and feels satisfied with seeing only the flower.
How, then, could yellow, asks the yellow one,
express yellow if, being a flower,
it should be expressing flower
the same way the red one does?
Maybe if it were magenta
it could be itself, like the red one is itself,
only more like a flower and not like red?
If the yellow flower could be a flower,
according to the red flower,
then the red one could accept
the yellow one as the same, like a flower,
and, therefore, define it as a flower
and not as a yellow flower, which isn't a red one.
Wouldn't that help make the red one
more comfortable not being a red flower
so that the red one could simply be a flower, too?

Lotus
Acrylics: 12x12

The Plastic Tongue

The scarred and tossed aside toy
still licks the air with its odd plastic
smile and rubber face. A young
imagination could have given
any definition it chose for it,
scraping it along endless boundaries
and then losing it when done
somewhere where it is set free
to dissolve its given shape
and become some melted thing of itself.

Money Toad
Pencil Drawing on paper

When History is Now

Reflections of history
from a year or a decade,
or a moment, somewhere
near the future, some time
that has not happened,
when the winds of disaster
unlock the clear doors,
and the landscapes and lots
show the scars of loss,
capture the beginning
and embalm it within masks
like sepia snapshots
resolving sorrows
still waiting to be faced.

Squoze
Acrylics: 16x20

Eyes

Yellow. Pinned
wherever they pierce
any passerby—

Sharp, like a sudden
awareness of being shocked
bare to the center of the soul
with no distracting thoughts
to hide behind—

Those eyes watch
long before they reveal
their glowing yellow
electric vibrations—
Impossible to escape
their witnessing!

CAT
Digital

Blue Cat

An empty Saturday, old songs echo in the chamber café.
Who might pull the door and have the hinges
grind an announcement like a potential break in the dull?
Another ghost blindly walking by silent voices of night's shadow,
eminent like a cape, all earth-stone faced.
Somewhere, a blue cat pads past a nightmare
to the twisted whirlpools of morning's light.

Liquids

Drink periwinkle!
Face down, the afternoon
that spreads last night's rain
into open petals
embeds its buggy
proboscis for a sup
of sappy sipping.

Bug
Digital

The Most Beautiful Fly in the World
Acrylics: 11x15

The Prints of Nighttime

About a minute before the rain
slowed to a sprinkle and a few
after that train horn sounded
loudly along the tracks
enough to drown any group
of teenagers standing near enough
to challenge it with their strongest
and most cathartic yawp,
the slow flowing soil
stopped next to the curb
and marked the signature of the night
with its quiet and delicate paws.

Spirit Fox
Acrylics: 16x20

The Lost Shoe

One shoe rests, checkered
and yielding at the foot of the sign
at the curbside on the corner
of a four-way intersection.
The child already reached
his or her dinner
and may have slipped
the match behind a crowd
of other shoes at the entrance
to avoid being asked,
"Why one bare foot?"
This lone shoe is done with walking.
It will not relent its story,
how it may or may not have
slung away from the pedal
of a bicycle, or slipped
off the child's foot
when he or she opened
the car door in the back seat,
awakened from a nap,
and believed he or she had arrived
and parked in the driveway.
The shoe yields for passersby
to move along and wonder
and nothing more.

A Mile in Boots (A Long Story)
Acrylics: 16x20

Tucked in the Corner of Red

At the street side, a mailbox
stands on the shoulder
guarded by a side rail.

The address marks an empty lot of grass.

No one can stop
to lower its door and deliver
a note to any residents.

The house belonging to that number
vanished a long time ago.

According to the red on the walls
of the shed tucked into the branches
that wrap it with the hidden slow time,
the decaying, fading echoes
of the shadow of Manor 904,
not even a driveway marks
a way to the entrance of its absence.

Street in China After Rain
Oil Pastels on Canvas: 24x30

The Missing Beam

The absence is so solid!
Strong enough, still, to support
the lives of the memories
under the roof of the porch
leaning like the walls inside
the empty rooms.
The tiles speak
of nights resisting
hailstorms and days
when the noon sun
wrinkled them with heat.
That door sits like a metal gate
locking in the invisible—
The missing beam
will never fall.

Can Yellow See Yellow?
for Brophew

The brilliant color
cannot see itself
breathing its light,
brilliant, abrupt,
and uninterrupted,
and how it stops
anyone who may stop
short one step
after hitting a wall
of yellow
solid like bricks.

Caterpillar
Acrylics: 16x20

The Day's Overtime

The day
lay its spoon
face down on the pavement,
the back like a funny mirror
for it to reflect into another hour,
reshaping the curve of the horizon
so that the sunlight might spread
into the arch of the rising moon,
its oranges and reds like flowers
blooming at the edges and from the cracks
of the random road at the foot of an ordinary hill.

Turtles at Rest

For when the day sighs
with relentless silence—
interrupted by the drop
of startled turtles
into glass-still water—
its shoulders,
sunning bare like cat tails,
drop the tension,
and its eyes
droop lightly
into a sunning doze.

A Box of Stillness
for Ripples

There, the day rediscovers
its nap in the light winds—
Only the sunlight reflects
any meaning in ripples
on the water.
Without a roof,
without a wall of hands and nails,
the day still believes
in holding the moment still.

Harbor Moon Café
Acrylics 24 x 36

From Squib to Flower

Since the subject has come up,
wildflowers struck from the rain-soaked
lawn like fireworks from tails
climbing slowly on top of linear sprouts
then bursting pink and yellow, always yellow,
and opening wide to swallow the color of the sun.

Too Hot
Acrylic Markers

Yawning in Yellow

Some mornings yawn
yellow from the freshly watered
jade, quietly and without
the pace of minutes,
with some slow speed of night
puzzling through memories
while swimming through dreams.

A Toad is Home

Next, after the toad smiles
comfortably nestled under wet soil,
night drops a light spore
in the pot with the jade,
furnishing the garden
with a moment of mushrooms.

Something Texas
Acrylics: 16x20

The Fish Sees Me, Too

How the fish sees me
while I wait in stillness
for a picture to capture
a day in the sun near the water
and in the raucous of the noisy geese,
and how the fish swims
a wide arch back to the cover
of the bank's small overhang,
and how we see each other
through the warped rippling
on the water, waves
from a vigorous duck bath,
and what the sunlight does
to the color of the sediment
and the way the fish adopts it in brown—
Motion under water sets the sun ready to spin.

A Fish
Pencil Drawing

Petals Paint the Sky

We stuck our days
between long hours
where they could sleep
and dream, perhaps,
of childhood play,
sliding down hills
on flat cardboard
pretending sunrises
and sunsets and yelling
in brilliant colors.

We tried catching them
in tiny gears and ribbons
of thin metal and calling them
seconds, minutes, hours.

They let us do that
to preoccupy ourselves
with our own sense
of progress and productivity
and to give ourselves means
to monitor each other.

Seems we forgot
without our markers
what light and dark does
to the subtle changes
birds and flowers sing.

They never stopped sliding.
They stuck out their tongues
like petals of Spring
and painted the sky with light.

Symbiosis

Symbiotic—three blooms
lick at the Spring's morning,
eating the yellow sunrise.

So many small porches!
Slow moments hiding under
unfolding petals—
thresholds of stillness…

Three timeless currents blossom
on one stem over eight eyes.

Look at that bead of water,
honeysuckle sap of the center
of the mandala of all that moves,

luring thirsty moths or newborn butterflies
to halt their jagged flights,
patterns of a leaf blown
by heated winds of afternoons,
and take a sip of its reflecting sunlight
gathered by the blossom's petals.

A Moth Sits on its Favorite Tomato
Acrylics: 16x20

Bees

So much to do
to work Spring
from the grey sky!

Bees seem so still, somehow,
while they float determined
in a singular task, greeting
each blossom as if coaxing
it gently from its hibernation.

Their dance of one yellow
to another fresh green
unfolds with the air
of their wingbeats
and their rapid, steady breathing.

Stinger
Alcohol Markers

Dew Drop

When I focused on the first, strong
drop of thick, black coffee, and I placed
my heavy, slow morning concentration
onto the eggs, the sausages, the cranberry bread,
and the rising hours of work,

something patient, timeless, unhurried
unfolded in between the thoughts
I had gripped so tightly like tools
to pound and to knead the future day.

The porch and the sunrise paid no attention
to outcome, due dates, presentations of success
within established parameters.

Below the limits of detection,
that line I want to catch
when I watch the sunrise,
as if I could see it if I were
to stare at it long enough,
a drop of dew rested jade blossom
on the petals of a jade plant,
stilled in all the minutes of the morning
unaware of the fresh steam from my cup.

Dare to Flame
Acrylics: 16x20

The Old Gate

This gate might grin, still,
on patches of grass, broken
like old teeth ready to crack
open and swallow anything
lost in thought and passing
by time slowly leaning
in those boards and braces
exposed in gaps of missing shingles.

Which window back there,
each like a socket without glass,
used to gaze at the road
and resist the rain
when moments danced
like flower petals
in the lawn of early Spring?

The gate holds time closed,
and those floors in those spaces
where there were rooms at night
fall through with the cracking
of the footsteps of each passing minute.

The Edge of Decay

The edge of sunset decays,
sliding through broken rooves
and filtering onto echoes
of voices in the patchy lawn.

The missing planks suggest
reflected porch light
when evening lit the end
of tired days and the beginning
of the soft creaking of night's sleep.

The lights' memory leans
against the framework's studs,
thin like the missing windows' curtains
and heavy like the dense breath of time.

A Cat Skull Full of Dead Flowers
Oil Pastels 18x24

The Butterfly Feast

In the crevices of the bark
seeps a sappy service
for the slurping sanguine
slurpers sipping slowly
sliding drops of satiating sap.

Butterflies bunch beautifully
on the benign bark bearing bounty
that begets unbundled proboscis

that pontificate and probe
the pumping of the plentiful
perhaps for no true plan
but to beholden to the kaleidoscope
and bear the feast of the butterfly.

Red Rabbit with Osprey Wings
Acrylics: 16x20

A Wish

A wish scratched in metal
and locked tightly within silence
bridges two whispers
before and after the key
reaches the bed and rests
on layers of hopes.

Coalescence
Acrylics: 24x36

The Bike

...and into the tires the pump
pushed new air, breathed life
into the evening when the heat
subsided to less than a stroke
of dehydration uphill...
...and ride to the park
with liquids and poetry
stuffed in a black backpack...
...and peddle hard in sandals
all four speeds, the last of its kind
before the brand closed...
...green like a memory
of a child within, and topped
with a bell to ring the path
ahead...
Soon! Ride! Soon!

Mirror

...and stopped, to reflect
the electric sky, the effects
of gyroscopes on gravity...

...the discarded reflection
near the edge of the road,
looking up, or looking into...

...who talks about mirrors
but misses the object...

...green frame, or the opposite
of a green frame, with shiny fenders...

...so much sky inside a black
frame crossed by bicycles and wire...

...almost as if the ground
has a hole in it that emits the sky...

...either the bike or the shadow
of the bike bouncing off the mirror...

...this one came with a kickstand,
and the unwanted mirror
still has a hook for a nail...

...transformer, transportation,
transition, translucence...

...position one, summer heat
stop for water, remove helmet;
position two, how do front doors
leak mirrors onto the street...

Money Tree
Acrylics: 16x20

Mike Matthews is a professor, published poet, and artist. His two books are titled, *Water of Joy*, and *Ashes*, both published by Finishing Line Press. He lives with his family in a small city, Copperas Cove, in Texas. He teaches college English courses including Creative Writing I Three Genre, Creative Writing II Novel Writing, and Literature for community college students in Killeen, Texas. He studied for his Masters of Fine Arts in Creative Writing, Poetry, in San Marcos, Texas, at Texas State, and he studied English, Music, and Fine Arts in undergrad school at the University of Texas at Austin. Mike Matthews' mediums include words, acrylics, oil pastels, and digital. After his classes are over and he is not busy revising or painting, Mike Matthews goes for walks to the pond in the park to practice listening for the whispers that manifest the moments of poetry and art.

www.ingramcontent.com/pod-product-compliance
Lightning Source LLC
Chambersburg PA
CBHW041941180426
43198CB00031B/114